The people were divided into two groups – free people and slaves. Slaves were owned by free people. They worked as servants and labourers. Citizens were wealthy free men. They took part in government and served in the army. Women looked after the house and family.

The ancient Greeks loved art and learning. They built magnificent temples and theatres. Many great thinkers, mathematicians and writers were Greek.

3

Greek writing

Only boys went to school. They wrote by scratching letters on to a wooden tablet covered in melted wax.

You will need:

Thick cardboard   Thin cardboard   Pencil
Wax crayons   Brown paint   Glue

Follow the steps . . .

1. Paint the thick cardboard brown to look like a wooden tablet.

2. Colour the thin cardboard with wax crayon. Completely cover the coloured crayon with black crayon. Glue the cardboard on to the tablet.

3. Use the pencil to scratch your name. Some Greek letters are shown opposite. There were no letters for C, F, H, J, Q, V, W, X, Y. Make up your own for these.

FOOTSTEPS

THE
Greeks

Sally Hewitt

Contents

3000 BC   2000 BC   1000 BC   0   1000 AD   2000 AD

Egyptians

Greeks

Romans

Vikings

W
FRANKLIN WATTS
LONDON · SYDNEY

Who were the Greeks?

Ancient Greece was a land of mountains, valleys and hundreds of islands. The cities were cut off from each other by the mountains. They traded with each other by sea. There was no king of the whole country. Cities ruled themselves, and some, like Athens and Sparta, became very rich and powerful.

Greece

Aegean Sea

Athens

Mediterranean Sea

Crete

α	β	γ	δ	ε	ζ	θ	ι	κ	λ	μ
a	b	g	d	e	z	th	i	k	l	m

ν	ο	π	ρ	ς	τ	υ	φ	χ	ψ
n	o	p	r	s	t	u	ph	ch	ps

Knucklebones

Girls stayed at home and learned how to run the house. They played a game called knucklebones.

You will need:

Newspaper   Bowl   Water

PVA glue   Paint

Follow the steps . . .

1. Put small pieces of newspaper into the bowl. Mix equal amounts of glue and water. Pour the mixture over the pieces to make papier mâché.

2. Squeeze the papier mâché into little knucklebone shapes. Let them dry. Paint them.

3. Throw the knucklebones into the air and try to catch them on the back of your hand.

Homes

The houses of wealthy city people were made of sun-dried mud bricks. The floors were made of beaten earth. Children played in a central courtyard which had an altar for family prayers and a well to supply water. Windows were small and high to keep out the heat, the noise and the smell of the streets. Men and women lived in separate parts of the house.

The men held parties for their friends. They lay on couches while slaves served them with food and drink.

Olive oil was used for washing. People rubbed it into their skin, scraped it off and splashed themselves with cold water from a large pot.

Vase decoration

Black-figure and red-figure vases were popular.
They were often decorated with stories of the gods.

You will need:

Black paper   Orange paper   Pencil
Scissors   Glue

Follow the steps . . .

1. Copy this vase shape.
   Cut out one black vase and two
   orange vases, exactly the same.

2. Draw a shape on to the black vase
   and cut it out. Glue the shape
   on to one of the orange vases.
   This is a black-figure vase.

3. Glue the rest of the black vase
   on to the other orange vase to
   make a red-figure vase.

Clay figures

We have learned about the everyday life of the ancient Greeks from the little clay figures they made.

You will need:

Modelling clay   Modelling tool   Water

Follow the steps . . .

1. Make a small ball of clay for the head, a fat roll for the body and long thin rolls for limbs.

2. Put the pieces together to make a figure. Dampen the parts you want to stick.

3. Bend the arms and legs. Make the hair and face with the modelling tool. Leave it to dry.

4. Make a model of yourself. Maybe someone will find it in 2,500 years!

A day at the theatre

During the five day festival of Dionysus in Athens, huge crowds filled the theatre. People brought a picnic and watched plays all day. Those who were too poor to pay were given free tickets.

Tragedies were serious plays which told stories of the gods and great heroes. Comedies were very funny, with jokes about politicians and well-known people.

Sport and games

Sport was very important in ancient Greece. It kept the young men fit and ready for war. The Olympic Games, held in honour of Zeus, were the biggest and most important games. Events included wrestling, chariot races, running and javelin throwing. Winners received an olive wreath, a palm branch and ribbons.

An Olympic torch

In the ancient Olympic Games, relay runners passed a torch to each other rather than a baton. The winner lit a fire to the gods.

You will need:

Newspaper   Sticky tape   Black paper

White, orange, yellow and red tissue paper

Follow the steps . . .

1. Cut out half a circle of black paper and roll it into a cone shape. Tape the edges together.

2. Crumple some newspaper into a ball. Cut the white tissue paper into strips. Cut the coloured tissue paper into flame shapes.

3. Push the ball of newspaper into the cone and tape the ends of the tissue paper on to it.

Theatre masks

All the actors were men. They wore masks with big, open mouths which made their voices louder.

You will need:

Cardboard	Newspaper	Scissors
String	Hole puncher	Wool
PVA glue	Paints and brush	

Follow the steps . . .

1. Copy the outline of the mask on to the cardboard. Cut it out. Punch holes in the tabs.

2. Dip small pieces of newspaper in a mixture of glue and water. Glue them all over the mask, especially near the eyebrows and mouth. Let the mask dry.

3. Paint the mask. Glue on wool for hair. Thread string through the tab holes.

Gods and legends

The Greeks believed that gods and goddesses watched over every part of their lives. The gods had to be pleased and obeyed. The Greeks made offerings to the gods outside the beautiful temples they built for them.

Zeus

Aphrodite

Hermes

Pluto

Athena

Hera

The most powerful gods were the twelve
Olympians who lived on cloud-covered Mount
Olympus. The father of the gods was called
Zeus. When he threw his spear, thunder crashed
and lightning flashed across the sky.

Medusa head

Greek legend said that people turned into stone if they looked at snake-haired Medusa the Gorgon.

You will need:

Coloured paper   Cardboard   Pencil   Crayons

Green tissue paper   Scissors   Glue   Foil

Follow the steps . . .

1. Cut 16 snakes out of coloured paper. Glue foil eyes and tongues on the snakes.

2. Curl the snakes by pulling a pair of closed scissors along the bodies.

3. Crumple a circle of tissue paper for Medusa's face. Glue it on to a circle of cardboard. Add eyes, a nose and a mouth.

4. Glue the snakes' tails around the edge of Medusa's head.

INDEX

Entries in *italics* are activity pages.

© 1995 Franklin Watts
This edition 2001

Franklin Watts
96 Leonard Street
London EC2A 4XD

Franklin Watts Australia
56 O'Riordan Street
Alexandria, Sydney
NSW 2015

ISBN 0 7496 4170 3

Dewey Decimal Classification
Number 938

A CIP catalogue record for this
book is available from the British
Library.

10 9 8 7 6 5 4 3 2

Editor: Annabel Martin
Consultant: Richard Tames
Design: Mike Davis
Artwork: Cilla Eurich
          Ruth Levy
Photographs: Peter Millard

Printed in Malaysia